BE MORE

DUA LIPA

CONTENTS

JUST START NOW... 4
Dua embodies positivity, manifestation, and self-belief—all things that ultimately helped her reach the stardom we see now. Take inspiration from Dua and make your dreams happen!

BLOW THEIR MINDS 16
Reaching your goals is one thing, maintaining that success is another. Dua has shown us the importance of leaning on others for help and persisting against obstacles that get in your way.

MAKE THE MOST OF LIFE 28
Don't be afraid to have fun and enjoy yourself. Dua knows how to be radically optimistic and live her life to the fullest. Learn to "Dance the Night Away" and bring positivity to every day!

BE OF SERVICE 40
Giving back to the world around us can enrich our lives. Whether it's offering your talents or speaking up about issues that matter, you can make a difference, just like Dua.

NEVER FORGET WHO YOU ARE 52
The essence of Dua comes from the people around her and everything she has been through. Like Dua, embrace nostalgia and reflect on what made you the person you are today.

INTRODUCTION

From singing in a television ad to headlining Glastonbury and a sell-out global arena tour, Dua Lipa's rise to fame has been stratospheric. Nowadays, you can find her hanging out with Elton John or Charli xcx, on billboards for the world's biggest fashion brands, and taking over the charts with her party-worthy bangers. However, it is no accident that Dua Lipa has achieved this success. She manifested her future—she's a savvy businesswoman who works hard until she gets it right and she has always stayed true to herself on the way to the top.

Known for her disco beats and infectious pop songs that make you want to get up and dance, this is an icon who lives and breathes positive energy. There's so much we can learn from this musical sensation—from her perseverance through setbacks to her dedication to promoting collaboration and community. Read on for 25 "New Rules" to help you do it like Dua and "Be the One" to live a life full of purpose and joy.

DISCLAIMER
This book has not been written or endorsed by Dua Lipa. It was created for Dua Lipa fans, by Dua Lipa fans. It is a love letter to Dua and all those who feel a connection to her.

CHAPTER 1

JUST START

NOW

If there's one thing we know about Dua, it's that she is a doer. For Dua, no dream is too far out of reach and nothing is impossible—not even winning countless awards, starring in movies, and headlining the biggest festivals in the world. Her secret? Believing it can happen and setting the wheels in motion to get there.

"As my dad likes to say, I'm a very hard person to say no to. I've always been very determined. I've always known what I wanted."

Just Start Now

GO GET 'EM!

Once upon a time, in the country of Kosovo, a 15-year-old girl called Dua, meaning "love" in Albanian, set out on a mission to achieve her wildest dreams. Having grown up listening to P!nk, Nelly Furtado, and Gwen Stefani, Dua imagined herself following in their footsteps. She hoped to become a sassy pop star, performing songs that young girls like her could relate, dance, and scream along to. And Dua was determined to make sure this became her reality. She convinced her parents to allow her to move back to London, her birthplace, to live with a family friend and pursue her singing career. Still a teenager, she had to balance her passion with her studies at school. Living miles away from home and managing her time at such a tender age can't have been easy for Dua, but it set her on the path she longed to go down. Sometimes we have to make scary moves to get us where we want to go. It's not always going to be easy, but it is usually worth it in the end.

"I stand very firmly in the belief of putting things into the world. Subconsciously, you just work towards them. Nothing's ever too big."

Just Start Now

MANIFEST IT

As soon as Dua started making music, she had one huge goal in mind: headlining at her favorite, and possibly the most famous, festival in the world: Glastonbury. To the average person, this probably seemed like an impossible feat. After all, the headline slot at Glastonbury is reserved for the greats. The festival has seen the likes of Beyoncé, David Bowie, and Paul McCartney as headliners. Fast-forward to 2024, and her dream became a reality. Dua credits this to "manifesting"—the idea of putting things out into the universe, whether that's writing down your dreams and aspirations or telling people what you want to happen in your future. If you do this, you'll subconsciously be working toward those goals, finding opportunities and pathways you might not have discovered otherwise. Whatever your goal, no matter how "ridiculous" it seems, follow Dua's rules and manifest the hell out of it.

"What's meant for me is for me."

Just Start Now

TRUST THE PROCESS

From the outside, it might seem like Dua exploded onto the music scene as a ready-made pop star in 2016. With the releases of her singles "Hotter Than Hell" and "Blow Your Mind (Mwah)," Dua immediately solidified her position as a successful artist dominating radio stations. But it wasn't exactly like that. Alongside studying and posting singing videos online, Dua made her way by waitressing, working in bars, and modeling. Although this was a lot for her to balance at the same time as her musical endeavors, Dua's hustling paid off and got her noticed. Aged 17, she landed a commercial for the talent show *The X Factor*. She sang Sister Sledge's "Lost in Music," which resulted in her first record deal. It might not feel like anything is happening, but then suddenly things start to fall into place. You never know where each step might lead. Just keep putting one foot in front of the other and watch all your hard work pay off.

"If you believe in yourself and you're proud of what you do, never let anyone tell you you're doing it wrong."

Just Start Now

BELIEVE IN YOURSELF

It's hard to imagine that anyone could criticize the quality of Dua's voice—it is rich, sultry, and controlled. Yet that is exactly what happened when she was at school in Kosovo. In an audition for the school choir, she recalls an attempt at a "crazy high note" where no noise came out. "The whole school started laughing, and [the teacher] said, 'Oh, better luck next time.'" For the average person, this kind of early rejection might have turned them away from singing for life. But not Dua Lipa. She has expressed her belief that "when you face rejection, you have to be the person that's going to support your dreams and your goals, and you have to pick yourself back up." So she kept singing, taking lessons in London, where she honed her craft and leaned into her powerful lower range. Just like Dua, you too should hold onto your belief in yourself. Be your own biggest cheerleader and don't let anything or anyone get in the way of your dreams. Having faith in your own abilities will get you far.

> **I really enjoy all the little things along the way, and see every baby step as a little victory.**

Just Start Now

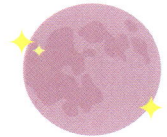

CELEBRATE THE SMALL WINS

Whether you're pursuing a passion or starting a new job, it can be very easy to load unnecessary pressure on yourself. Thoughts like *I should have reached my goal by now* and *Why is it taking so long to get the hang of this?!* can dominate your mind. But do as Dua does and take stock of every win along the way. Even feeling more in control than you did yesterday is a win. Meeting a new person who could help you on your journey, that's a win. Coming up with an awesome new idea, even if you haven't started it yet, that's a win. If your focus is solely on the end goal, you can unintentionally overlook all the excitement and joy that has been around you the whole way through the process. And if you keep celebrating those baby steps, you might soon find yourself celebrating GRAMMY awards or sharing the stage at the Royal Albert Hall with Elton John. You never know!

CHAPTER 2
BLOW THEIR
MINDS

When your hard work starts to take you down the path of success, superstardom can arrive suddenly—but it can also be fleeting. Dua Lipa knows the way to maintain this is through tenacity, hard work, and making sure she is surrounding herself with the right people. Channeling Dua's drive can help you push boundaries and make a lasting impression on others.

"Nothing is given, and nothing is taken for granted. Everything I want and everything I have; I've worked really hard to get there."

WORK HARD

Before Dua was born, her parents lived in Kosovo. They made the decision to flee the war-torn country in search of a safer life, leaving their flourishing careers behind. Restarting their lives in London wasn't easy, and they made their way by working in restaurants and bars while studying in their spare time, eventually transitioning into jobs in marketing and tourism. Little Dua watched her parents work hard to achieve the life they wanted, and she inherited their tenacity and resilience. "My work ethic is an immigrant work ethic," she has said. "I feel like I need to work really hard to get where I want to be." You can see this in every single thing Dua does, from the way she pores over her songs, perfecting them until they're just right, to the way she rehearses for her performances until they are second nature. Dua—and her parents—are living proof that you can start with nothing and turn it into gold; it's just going to take some grit.

> "I like to prove that I can do it. I'm stubborn."

Blow Their Minds

PROVE THEM WRONG

The 2018 BRIT Awards marked a huge turning point in Dua's career—and not because she won two highly coveted awards. After the performance of her smash hit "New Rules," she was criticized for her lack of stage presence. One comment on YouTube read, "I love her lack of energy, go girl give us nothing!" which spawned a viral meme. Understandably, this was extremely hurtful for our young pop star, who later described the experience as "humiliating." But it was also, possibly, one of the best things that happened to her. Seeing the criticism lit a fire inside Dua to prove her haters wrong. And a year later, the time and energy Dua had spent working on her stage presence and live act was evident in her performance of "Don't Start Now" at the MTV EMAs. "Maybe I thrive on being undermined," she said. Now, she's known as one of the best pop performers of our generation, a star who truly gives us everything. It just shows that even the harshest critiques don't have to tear us down, and instead we can use them as fuel to unlock our highest potential.

"Writing is definitely not easy, but when you do it with people who allow you to be yourself, you really get the best out of it."

Blow Their Minds

COLLABORATE

Have you ever heard the first few bars of a song and instantly felt the need to get up and dance? If "One Kiss" by Calvin Harris and Dua Lipa springs to mind, then you're definitely not alone. With Calvin's flair for catchy, sparkly beats and Dua's sultry pop influence, it's no wonder that their collaborative hit became one of the songs of the summer in 2018. Dua's own musical process tends to involve close collaboration with songwriters and producers, including Tame Impala's Kevin Parker. This extends to other artists' discographies, with Dua sharing song credits with Miley Cyrus, JENNIE, and Elton John. Outside the recording studio, Dua's performances often include surprise guests. The Radical Optimism Tour saw a local artist making an appearance at each show, with Charli xcx joining her on stage in London and Troye Sivan sharing the mic in Melbourne. Dua proves that when we share the stage with others, we strengthen our own skills and allow their talents to shine brightly, too. Collaboration and the mutual goal of creating something should not be underestimated. Together, we are unstoppable.

"When you know your worth, you know what you want and what you don't want."

Blow Their Minds

KNOW YOUR WORTH

There's a common theme running throughout many of Dua's hits. In "Houdini," she explains that she'll only stick around for a romantic partner who makes the effort and is good enough for her. In "Training Season," Dua sings about wanting someone who already knows how to be a good partner for her, not someone she has to teach—we've all been there! These songs are all about knowing your worth and your value in romantic relationships. They're about understanding what you bring to the table and not putting up with crumbs from your partner, especially since you deserve the whole cake! These are important lessons for all of us, and they're not just applicable to romance. When it comes to friendship and work, you deserve to be respected, valued, and appreciated. No more shrinking into the background and letting people walk all over you—because training season is well and truly over.

"You have to go through the bad things to get to the good part."

Blow Their Minds

ROLL WITH THE PUNCHES

Life can never be just sunshine, rainbows, and butterflies, not even for a global sensation like Dua Lipa. She has been through her fair share of hard times, from challenging relationships and agonizing breakups to relentless criticism and pressures from an industry that expects women to act a certain way. Yet Dua's attitude is that all the bad things are there for a reason—they force us to retreat, to reassess, and to remind us of the things we really care about and what we really want. Through all the hard times she has also learned an important lesson: that it's okay not to be okay. It's okay to not be strong all the time and to take each day as it comes. Being patient with yourself and giving yourself grace will allow time for you to figure out how to get through these tough situations. And once those wounds have healed, you can come back ready to blow everybody's minds with even more joy and electricity than ever.

CHAPTER 3
MAKE THE
MOST OF LIFE

From traveling the globe, to reading insightful novels, to dancing in nightclubs, Dua lives and breathes the "work hard, play hard" mentality. Maximizing the joy in your life makes everything a whole lot easier. After all, what's the point in all that hard work if we don't get to let loose and enjoy ourselves?

"In order to work and take care of me, I like to plan things. That way, I can do it all."

Make the Most of Life

ORGANIZE YOUR LIFE

Are you the kind of person who can't live without your to-do list? If so, you're just like Dua Lipa. And if not, this could become your new happiness hack. Our sparkly pop star is known for being hyper-organized. "I'm obsessed with my schedule," she has explained. "I put in 'have a shower' and 'get ready.' Everything is down to the minute." This level of planning might seem like overkill, but really, it ends up saving time in the long run. For someone as busy as Dua, planning everything so meticulously allows her to be efficient with her time. And when this level of organization is applied to your everyday life, you get more done in a shorter window. More time is left free for the things, places, and people you love, and there is more time for you to relax and enjoy. It's genius, really. So take your schedule seriously, and you'll make the most of every waking moment.

"I love being on the dance floor, and being the first on the dance floor if nobody else is dancing."

Make the Most of Life

DANCE THE NIGHT AWAY

Dua Lipa might be known for creating the kind of bangers that get you up on your feet, whether you're at a party or in your very own living room, but she doesn't just *make* this kind of music. She actively lives and breathes the dance scene. Dua loves to rave in Ibiza, get right into the Glasto crowds, and hit a nightclub wherever she is—another quality she inherited from her fun-loving parents. And why does she love it so much? "In a crowd, you share this common language. It's so fun and joyous ... that connection you have with the complete stranger next to you." Being in a crowd of people with that same interest creates a sense of belonging and joy in a way nothing else can. And this can definitely be said for a Dua Lipa concert. You are connected to every single person in that room, including Dua, with a collective passion for great songs and letting loose. Dancing with others is the ultimate way to shake off your inhibitions and truly feel alive. May we all take a leaf out of Dua's book and dance our way through life.

"I like to be out of my comfort zone."

Make the Most of Life

SEEK NEW EXPERIENCES

Our girl loves to travel. Fans even dubbed her the "Vacanza Queen" because she always seems to be on vacation in between tour dates, from Ibiza to India. Dua takes the time to travel when she can because, as well as offering some much-deserved rest, it exposes her to new experiences, new cultures, and new ways of life. Stepping outside of your everyday routine is such a powerful way to expand your sense of self. But Dua doesn't only step outside of her comfort zone in terms of time and place—she also does it in her work. Starting her podcast, *Dua Lipa: At Your Service*, in 2022 was a leap into the unknown. Interviewing people, rather than being the interviewee, was a big departure from what she was used to and what was expected from her.

But she went ahead and did it anyway, teaching us that it's always rewarding to try something new, because that's the way to grow and expand. Being exposed to new things is one of the best ways to learn more about yourself. And anyway, you very rarely regret the things you do, but rather the things you don't do.

"I like to believe in magic. I feel like there's magic in everything."

Make the Most of Life

BE RADICALLY OPTIMISTIC

Radical Optimism is not just the name of Dua Lipa's third album, it is also a mantra she lives her life by. But what does it mean? It's all about embracing positivity, even when it feels like the world is crumbling around you. Dua has explained that it's "the idea of going through chaos gracefully and feeling like you can weather any storm." Rather than choosing to ignore the inevitable challenges, setbacks, and heartbreaks that being a human entails, a radically optimistic attitude incorporates a sense of calm and acceptance when things don't work out. It can make things that initially seemed insurmountable much easier to face head-on. After all, there is nothing more powerful than hope. Life can feel magical when you strive for happiness and trust that something good is around the corner. Adopting a positive outlook while accepting that things may not always be perfect can make all the difference to your life. Be radically optimistic, and you'll always find your way to the brighter side of life.

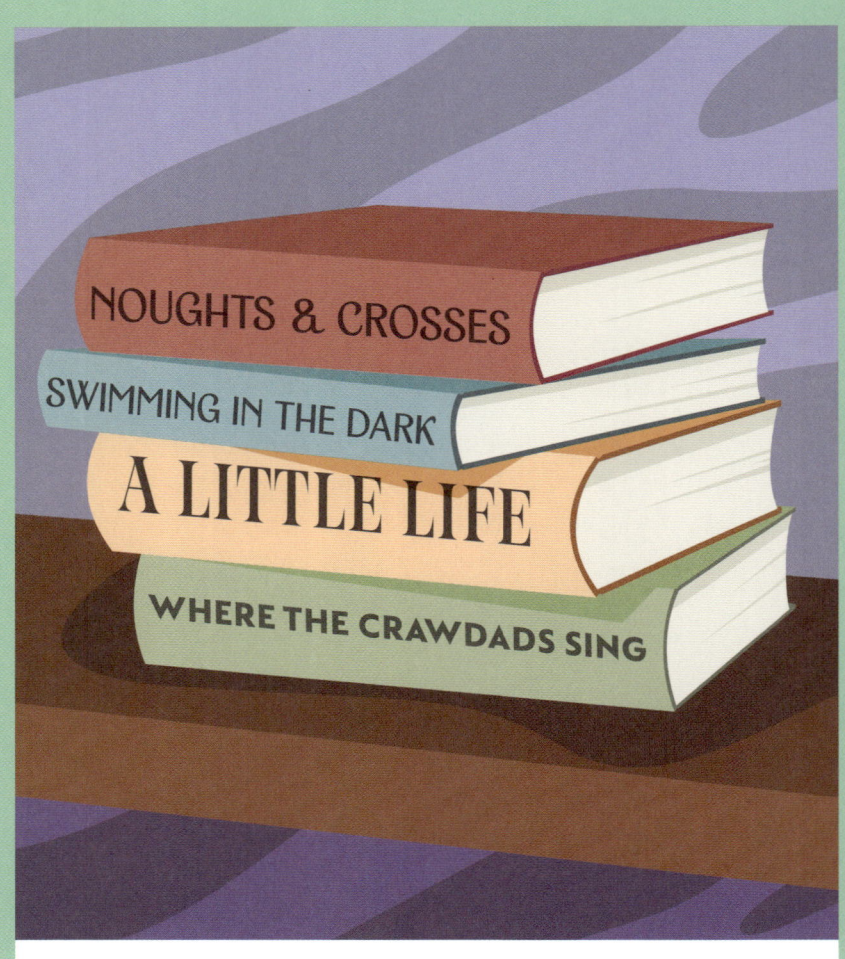

"One of the most profound joys in the world [is] the simple pleasure of reading a book."

Make the Most of Life

HAVE FUN WITH YOUR HOBBIES

You might not expect a pop powerhouse to be a bona fide bookworm, but Dua constantly defies expectations! She shouts loudly about her love of books, and among her favorites are modern novels including *Shuggie Bain* by Douglas Stuart, *A Little Life* by Hanya Yanagihara, *The Bee Sting* by Paul Murray, *Three Women* by Lisa Taddeo, and *Crying in H Mart* by Michelle Zauner. Add all of these to your reading list immediately, by the way. Dua loves reading because she can delve into new worlds (remember we said she loves being outside of her comfort zone? Reading is one of the ways she does that!). Even though it's often considered a solitary activity, Dua decided to have more fun with reading and started her very own book club. This meant she could share her passion and let others express the joy it brings them, too. Whatever your hobbies, whatever makes your heart sing, shout about it from the rooftops, get your friends involved, and make it a key part of your personality. Life is short—*so why the hell not?*

CHAPTER 4

BE OF

SERVICE

Dua is one of the most famous women on the planet, and she regularly uses this platform as an opportunity to give back. Whether that's brightening someone's day with a glittery pop anthem or drawing attention to war and famine around the world, Dua's morals have never left her side. We can all learn from her dedication to helping others.

"I love the idea that music lives in a fantasy, separated from the real world."

Be of Service

SPREAD POSITIVITY

Picture the following. It's March 2020. A virus called COVID-19 is rapidly spreading around the world, causing a global lockdown. Gatherings are prohibited, meaning no parties, no concerts, and definitely no clubs and festivals. Life as we know it has been put on pause. Meanwhile, Dua's second album, *Future Nostalgia*, is scheduled to be released. The advice is to delay it, as the timing is far from ideal. But what does Dua do? She puts her new, upbeat pop songs out into the world, completing her press tour over Zoom. And thank goodness for that decision—because we plugged into those vibrant songs on our daily walks, or invented dance routines in our kitchens. Even though Dua couldn't give us the full album experience that we are used to, she gave us exactly what we needed to get through those early days of quarantine. Sharing positivity is the easiest way to give back. So make people laugh, offer smiles and reassurance, and sprinkle good vibes like glitter wherever you go.

"Here's to more women on these stages, more women winning awards, and more women taking over the world."

Be of Service

DO IT FOR THE GIRLS

In the music video for her breakout single, "New Rules," we see Dua relying on an army of friends to help her get over a breakup. They make sure she sticks to her own rules and doesn't run back to her ex. That video was so iconic because it was so relatable—we have all had to look to our girlfriends for accountability, honesty, and comfort at some point in our lives. For Dua, her gal pals mean everything to her. She has expressed the important place that women hold in her life: "I always feel it's easier to talk to girls and I'm more open around female energy." And this translates to her professional life, too; we have seen Dua collaborate with so many brilliant women, including Charli xcx, BLACKPINK, and Julia Michaels. Dua is proof that when we hold out our hands to other women and support each other through feminine energy and empowerment, incredible things can happen.

"I think it's important to talk about your emotions and to be vulnerable and to show that you're human."

Be of Service

OPEN YOUR HEART

Generally, Dua's music focuses on empowerment and positivity. However, too much positivity, especially when it is forced, can be toxic, and it's important to admit when things are hard and sad. Difficult times are a reality of life, and these moments form an essential part of what makes us human. "These Walls" is about the denial that can come before the inevitable end of a relationship. Dua sings about knowing it's falling apart but neither person being willing to cut it off, and the complex feelings that come with this. It's such a relatable story for so many of us; heartbreak is encroaching, but you're not sure if you can face it. The truth is, love is complicated, and it's normal to face indecision and uncertainty. Dua sharing her own struggles through her music shows us that we are not alone. When we talk about these vulnerable, tender moments with each other, we realize that we can get through tough times. And being able to relate to others and see that they were able to overcome similar hardships can often provide clarity to our own personal challenges.

"I've always wanted to learn new things and dive in and find out about a book, or what's happening in different parts of the world."

Be of Service

KEEP LEARNING

For Dua Lipa, life is like one big classroom. The launch of her podcast, *Dua Lipa: At Your Service*, was driven by the desire to learn from fascinating people with unique perspectives on life. As the podcast name suggests, Dua has longed to share the information and knowledge available to her with others. And she was able to expand her audience further with the launch of her cultural lifestyle platform, *Service95*. This space was created to collate a vast range of information in one place, from the best places to eat in Madrid to the importance of diverse representation in the TV and film industry. Clearly, Dua has a hunger for absorbing new information, and this is one of her best qualities. After all, knowledge is power. The more we know, the more we not only enrich our lives, but are also armed with the information and empathy to do more for the world we live in. Learning is a massive strength, so stay open, stay curious, and learn something new every day.

"I feel very close to [those suffering] injustices in the world, or inequality. Whether that be war, or coming out to your family, everyone's got a different experience ... It's about support and learning together."

Be of Service

SPEAK UP AND BE COUNTED

In the pop world, there's often an expectation that stars sing their songs and then stay quiet about what's going on in the world. But Dua Lipa has never been an ordinary pop star. She has always spoken up for what she believes in—even if it's controversial or unpopular. Having grown up hearing stories of war and terror from her parents, it's understandable that Dua has always felt so close to people who are suffering or displaced. Her upbringing is one of the reasons that she has never allowed herself to stay silent. Through her platform *Service95* and by expressing her own views on social media, Dua has both backed and criticized politicians and raised awareness about countless important global causes, including wars, women's rights, LGBTQIA+ rights, and refugees. Fighting for what you believe in can be risky, but it's worth it to help make the world a better place. Change has to start somewhere, and speaking up is a great place to begin.

CHAPTER 5

NEVER FORGET

WHO YOU ARE

No matter how successful she has become, Dua has always kept her feet firmly on planet Earth. This is helped by staying close to her heritage, her family, and the things that make Dua feel truly herself. Wherever life takes you, you can always stay connected to who you really are.

> **It's important to remember where you're from; to do your part to try and give back.**

Never Forget Who You Are

LOVE YOUR HERITAGE

She might be one of the "It Girls" of pop, but Dua is also unwaveringly and unashamedly a girl from Kosovo. Throughout her ascent to stardom, our girl has always reflected on where she came from and paid homage to her roots. In 2016, she and her dad set up the Sunny Hill Foundation, a charity organization based in Pristina, Kosovo's capital city, designed to help those most in need and to inspire young people through arts and music. The organization also launched the biggest festival in Kosovo, Sunny Hill Festival, which has seen performances from Miley Cyrus to Stormzy to Calvin Harris and, of course, Dua Lipa. Her passion for her homeland is something that can inspire us all—no matter where we're from. Think about where, who, and what feels like home to you. Figuring these things out can inspire you to support and give back to the community that made you the incredible person you are.

"I'm so close with my family and my siblings. We're such a unit, which is really fun ... They keep me the most grounded. They give me normalcy."

Never Forget Who You Are

PUT FAMILY FIRST

It might not sound particularly glamorous to say, but being a pop star is a business. There are tours to organize, merchandise to sell, and brand deals to broker. And for Dua, her stardom is a family business. After she split from her management company in 2022, Dua's father, Dukagjin, took over as her manager. For her, this is a perfect arrangement since she knows she's working with someone who truly has her best interests at heart. But it's not all business meetings in the Lipa household. Dua, her parents, and her younger siblings, Rina and Gjin, frequently jet off on vacation together, and you can usually find them in the crowd at her shows, cheering her on. Whatever family means to you—whether it's blood or chosen—we all need our village to rely on. We all need those people who know us inside out to applaud us through the good and help us through the bad. Whoever those people are for you, hold them close and never take them for granted.

**"I love a trip down memory lane.
Looking back at photos and wondering what
that Dua would've thought of me now."**

Never Forget Who You Are

EMBRACE NOSTALGIA

Some people say you should always keep your eyes fixed on the future, pushing forward and focusing on your goals. But Dua knows the importance of looking back at the past, too. When you reflect on the different versions of yourself, you can see just how far you've come, how much you've learned, and how much you've changed for the better. Even when you feel like you haven't yet achieved everything you planned to, there are so many benefits to acknowledging that you've actually come a long way. You should use these moments as an opportunity to congratulate yourself and celebrate your progress. Ask yourself: "What would the younger version of me think of who I have become?" For Dua, that kid who was rejected from the choir would probably be both dumbfounded and starstruck. Guaranteed, the younger version of you would think you're pretty amazing. Reminiscing about your past and striving to achieve your ambitions can happen simultaneously, and both things are beneficial to your future.

"You have to be your own number one fan."

Never Forget Who You Are

BE YOUR OWN BEST FRIEND

We know Dua is a big fan of manifesting. This doesn't only apply to speaking her dreams into existence, it also applies to the way she talks to herself. "We've got to be careful about what we say to ourselves because we end up believing it," she has said, explaining her own inner monologue. "The more nice things we say to ourselves, the more that becomes the mantra we want to channel." Essentially, if you tell yourself you're a failure and unworthy, then that's how you'll feel and that's how you will inadvertently present yourself to others. But if you tell yourself that you're more than enough as you are and that you can achieve anything you set your mind to, then your mindset will begin to switch to a positive one. Ultimately, you need to speak to yourself like you'd speak to a friend. Be the most positive, reassuring, and encouraging version of yourself—because that's what friends do for each other. If you can't be that person in the front row cheering yourself on, then how can you expect anyone else to do that? It starts with you.

"I love my music career and the fact that it gives me so much opportunity for expression. But it's not the only thing I am."

Never Forget Who You Are

YOU GET TO DECIDE

Sure, Dua is best known as a pop star. But she's so much more than that. She's a model, a writer, an activist, a business owner, a podcast host, an actor … and who knows what she will be next? Dua is proof that you never have to be defined as just one thing—you can always open yourself up to new opportunities and adventures. There's a tendency to believe that once we have chosen our paths, we cannot deviate, and we have no choice but to stick to them. But that couldn't be further from the truth. It doesn't matter if you have always had one career or one hobby—you can continue to expand, grow, and try something different. You can always take a diversion. You get to decide who you are and who you become. You hold the keys to your future and your potential. Whatever you land on, throw your whole self into it, express yourself, and have a (disco) ball.

Editors Millie Acers, Sophie Dryburgh
Designer Isabelle Merry
Senior Production Editor Jennifer Murray
Senior Production Controller Louise Minihane
Senior Acquisitions Editor Pete Jorgensen
Managing Art Editor Jo Connor
Art Director Charlotte Coulais
Publisher Paula Regan
Managing Director Mark Searle

Written by Arielle Steele
Cover and interior illustrations Nastka Drabot
Additional artwork Isabelle Merry

DK would like to thank Julia March and Kayla Dugger for proofreading.

First published in Great Britain in 2026 by
Dorling Kindersley Limited
20 Vauxhall Bridge Road,
London SW1V 2SA

The authorised representative in the EEA is
Dorling Kindersley Verlag GmbH. Arnulfstr. 124,
80636 Munich, Germany

Copyright © 2026 Dorling Kindersley Limited
A Penguin Random House Company
10 9 8 7 6 5 4 3 2 1
001–355647–Feb/2026

All rights reserved.
No part of this publication may be reproduced, stored in or introduced into a retrieval system, or transmitted, in any form, or by any means (electronic, mechanical, photocopying, recording, or otherwise), without the prior written permission of the copyright owner.
DK values and supports copyright. Thank you for respecting intellectual property laws by not reproducing, scanning or distributing any part of this publication by any means without permission. By purchasing an authorised edition, you are supporting writers and artists and enabling DK to continue to publish books that inform and inspire readers.
No part of this publication may be used or reproduced in any manner for the purpose of training artificial intelligence technologies or systems. In accordance with Article 4(3) of the DSM Directive 2019/790, DK expressly reserves this work from the text and data mining exception.

A CIP catalogue record for this book
is available from the British Library.
ISBN: 978-0-2417-8544-7

Printed and bound in China

www.dk.com

Quotations: **p.6** "'When I became a meme it was humiliating and hurtful': Dua Lipa on pop, psychedelics and proving her haters wrong", *The Guardian*, Simon Hattenstone, 2024; **p.8** "Dua Lipa Manifested All of This", *Time*, Rachel Brodsky, 2024; **p.10** "Dua Lipa: 'Radical Optimism', Songwriting & Headlining Glastonbury", *Apple Music*, Zane Lowe, 2024; **p.12** "The Wylde Interview: Dua Lipa", *Wylde*, Philip Goodfellow, 2019; **p.13** "Trixie and DUA LIPA Practice the Art of Radical Optimism", *Trixie Mattel*, Trixie Mattel, 2024; **p.13** "Dua Lipa: 'Training Season' was Inspired by a 'Bad Date'", *The Drew Barrymore Show*, Drew Barrymore, 2024; **p.14** "Dua Lipa on leaving bad relationships and choosing Radical Optimism", *Q with Tom Power*, Tom Power, 2024; **p.18** "Dua Lipa on leaving bad relationships and choosing Radical Optimism", *Q with Tom Power*, Tom Power, 2024; **p.19** "Dua Lipa on leaving bad relationships and choosing Radical Optimism", *Q with Tom Power*, Tom Power, 2024; **p.20** "I'm Always Like, 'OK, What's Next?'": The Unstoppable Rise of Dua Lipa", *British Vogue*, Yomi Adegoke, 2021; **p.21** "Dua Lipa Is Done Being a Mystery", *Rolling Stone*, Brittany Spanos, 2024; **p.22** "Dua Lipa: The Music Week Interview", *Music Week*, Ben Homewood, 2024; **p.24** "Dua Lipa: 'If It's Not Fun, I Don't Want It'", *Elle*, Suzy Exposito, 2024; **p.26** "Dua Lipa: 'Training Season' was Inspired by a 'Bad Date'", *The Drew Barrymore Show*, Drew Barrymore, 2024; **p.30-31** "Dua Lipa on Her Very Detailed Daily Schedule, Notebook of Song Lyrics, New Album & Albanian Sayings", *Jimmy Kimmel Live*, Jimmy Kimmel, 2024; **p.32** "Dua Lipa Is Done Being a Mystery", *Rolling Stone*, Brittany Spanos, 2024; **p.33** "Dua Lipa on leaving bad relationships and choosing Radical Optimism", *Q with Tom Power*, Tom Power, 2024; **p.34** "I MET DUA LIPA", *Bru On The Radio*, Josh Brubaker, 2023; **p.36** "Dua Lipa interview: 'I feel like there's magic in everything'", *Popjustice*, 2016; **p.37** "Dua Lipa Unveils Title and Oceanic Cover of Her Upcoming Third Album 'Radical Optimism'", *People*, Jack Irvin, 2024; **p.38** "Dua Lipa's Booker Prize Speech: 'I wonder if authors realise how many gifts they give us'", *The Booker Prize Foundation*, 2022; **p.42** "Dua Lipa: the pop star turned tycoon on immigration, books—and men", *The Times*, Tim Cook, 2023; **p.44** "Brit awards 2018: Dua Lipa's speech after winning award for British female solo artist", *Guardian News*, 2018; **p.45** "Dua Lipa says she wants to work with more female producers", *NME*, Matthew Neale, 2020; **p.46** "Dua Lipa Is Ready For the Party On the Other Side", *Elle*, Melissa Giannini, 2020; **p.48** "Dua Lipa: 'Radical Optimism', Songwriting & Headlining Glastonbury", *Apple Music*, Zane Lowe, 2024; **p.50** "Dua Lipa: If It's Not Fun, I Don't Want It", *Elle*, Suzy Exposito, 2024; **p.54** "The Realest It Gets: Dua Lipa", *Clash*, Felicity Martin, 2017; **p.56** "Dua Lipa | Radical Optimism, Illusion, Manifestation", *Zach Sang Show*, Zach Sang, 2024; **p.58** "Dua Lipa on Glastonbury, gay best friends and who she's become", *i-D*, Douglas Greenwood, 2024; **p.60** "Dua Lipa: 'Training Season' was Inspired by a 'Bad Date'", *The Drew Barrymore Show*, Drew Barrymore, 2024; **p.61** "Dua Lipa: 'Training Season' was Inspired by a 'Bad Date'", *The Drew Barrymore Show*, Drew Barrymore, 2024; **p.62** "Dua Lipa Manifested All of This", *Time*, Rachel Brodsky, 2024.

This book was made with Forest Stewardship Council™ certified paper – one small step in DK's commitment to a sustainable future.
Learn more at www.dk.com/uk/information/sustainability

MIX
Paper | Supporting responsible forestry
FSC™ C018179